50 Fun & Easy

BRaiN-Based Activities

for Young Learners

by Ellen Booth Church

with a foreword by Bruce Perry, M.D., Ph.D

SCHOLASTIC
PROFESSIONAL BOOKS

New York • Toronto • London • Auckland • Sydney
Mexico City • New Delhi • Hong Kong • Buenos Aires

*To my best friend, Bernadette Fiocca,
whose commitment to understanding
the mind and body has taught me
to look deeper and grow.*

Cover art by Bari Weisman

Cover and interior design by Sydney Wright

Interior art by James Hale

ISBN: 0-439-20109-8

Copyright © 2002 by Ellen Booth Church
All rights reserved. Printed in the U.S.A.

3 4 5 6 7 8 9 10   40   08 07 06 05 04 03

Contents

Foreword

The human brain—what a masterpiece of biology! More than ten trillion cells are organized to communicate in ways that allow an individual to walk, talk, think, laugh, love and create. In ways mysterious and wonderful, our humanity emerges from these three pounds of fat, protein and water.

At birth this potential is unexpressed in the infant's undeveloped brain. The adaptive malleability of the brain—the capacity to change in response to patterned and repetitive experience—allows each child to develop a set of capabilities which suit his or her world. The Inuit child learns to understand the Inuit language, to read the stars for direction, and to recognize the subtle changes in wind which predict snow. The Japanese child learns to understand Japanese, to make a gentle curve with brush and ink to paint the symbols of the language, and to appreciate the value of group activities and objectives. The American child learns English, develops a proud sense of individualism and independence, and rapidly acquires the capacity to make very fine motor manipulations with a joystick to control an image on a video game screen! Each of these unique capacities requires that a unique pattern of neural systems organize and work together; at birth, the brains of all three children were capable of making all of these systems—yet it was the patterned, repetitive activities of each child that gradually shaped the neural systems of his or her brain in a slightly different way. Experience unveils and shapes the brain's remarkable potential.

This book outlines a set of activities to do just that. It provides specific ways to be involved with children and provide patterned, repetitive activities to help them "exercise" and develop specific brain-mediated capabilities. These activities require no special videos, no computer simulations, no technological devices, and no fancy props or specially-patented, "if-you-only-had-this-device" gimmicks. The activities in this book recognize and celebrate the responsiveness of the human brain to real human activities.

Our brain is the product of thousands of generations of adaptation. It is designed to be shaped by human experiences—safe, repetitive, interesting and rewarding experiences. Despite all the changes across the centuries, the properties of the developing brain and the true needs of children have not changed. So, as you engage in the activities in this book—as simple and playful as they seem—be assured that you are helping children unveil and develop the brain-mediated skills that will help them thrive in our complex and rapidly changing world.

—Bruce D. Perry, M.D., Ph.D

About This Book

As teachers, we support the growth and development of children's minds through stimulating activities that are fun and meaningful. We have always believed in the importance of quality, hands-on activities. We have seen with our own eyes the effect these activities have on children's development, their joy of discovery and mastery pushing them to the next level. We have seen the fun of learning reflected in children's faces. We have seen children blossom in the warmth of our supportive environments and caring attention. We have seen children's eyes shine when we take the time to talk with them.

Continuing research into how the brain develops in the first years of life supports what we have always known about the importance of hands-on activities and stimulating environments for young children—that multisensory, exploration-based activities are best for brain development. Music, physical movement, and sensory activities are not just add-on frills to basic curriculum but are actually core experiences that help the brain make sense of the enormous amount of information it receives every second.

At birth, an infant's brain has 100 billion neurons. The ways in which these neurons will connect depends in part on timing, nature, and the quality and quantity of experiences the child has over the next several years. Research has shown an important correlation between stimulating activities and healthy brain development. Early experience with learning materials and creative projects actually promotes synaptic growth and increases the brain's functional capacity. The activities in this book will help you support healthy brain development!

—*Ellen Booth Church*

BRAIN NEWS

- Repetitive use of materials with slight variations facilitates healthy brain development.

- Focused attention is necessary for learning, and children attend to an activity when it's both interesting and meaningful.

- Learning-based, nurturing relationships with adults support brain development.

- Physical exercise is important for healthy brain development.

- Novelty or change in environment, materials, or activities helps children make new synaptic connections.

- Music engages both the left and right hemispheres of the brain and stimulates abstract-reasoning skills.

- Small muscle movements encourage spatial-reasoning skills.

Changing the Variable

Each of the 50 activities in this book includes a section on ways to vary the activity. Studies in neuroscience tell us that frequent change of materials, experiences, and environment provide novelty for the brain, and that attention is naturally drawn to things unusual or new. Therefore, it is important to take a familiar (or newly acquired) activity and apply it to new situations or materials. In science, this is called "changing the variable." This provides not only novelty but important opportunities for practice and application. Doing activities in different ways also invites children to use flexible and fluent thinking skills. These skills help children see various possibilities, or view objects or situations in many different ways. Researchers have found that the ability to think flexibly and fluently is one of the most important skills for school success.

Children attend best when asked to use different parts of the brain in concert to grasp or learn new things. Looking at the same issue from a variety of perspectives, and varying the way in which you look at the same concept, keeps children's attention.

> *Words are a lens to focus one's mind.*
> —Ayn Rand
>
> ....
>
> *A mind that is stretched to a new idea never returns to its original dimension.*
> —Oliver Wendell Holmes

THINKING AND FEELING

The important "sister" skill to thinking is feeling. Positive emotions help the brain remember and integrate new information. Activities that invite children to feel and express emotions inspire these connections. In fact, it is often through our feeling nature that our greatest truths and understanding come! Have you ever had the experience of feeling something in your heart so strongly that you just knew it was right? As humans, we are a combination of emotional mind and rational mind. These two "minds" work in tight harmony to create our experience of life. Invite children to express how they feel, and offer a nonjudgmental environment in which children can take risks.

Brain-Boosting Skills

- **Observing:** watching, examining, gathering information

- **Comparing:** noticing similarities and differences

- **Predicting/Estimating:** speculating outcome, educated guessing

- **Classifying:** sorting objects and ideas into a variety of categories or sets

- **Matching:** putting similar objects and ideas together

- **Sequencing:** organizing objects in a row or series based on size or time

- **Patterning:** creating a repeating linear design such as ABAB

- **Determining cause and effect:** reaching logical conclusions based on experience

- **Inferring:** reaching logical conclusions from given or assumed evidence

- **Deducing:** reasoning from the general to the specific

- **Problem solving:** defining a problem, analyzing possible solutions, then choosing one and taking action upon it

- **Creative thinking:** brainstorming, using materials in different ways

- **Flexible thinking:** looking at things and ideas in new ways

- **Perceptual-motor:** taking in and processing information through body movement

- **Expressive and receptive language:** speaking and understanding spoken language

- **Sensory-motor:** taking in and processing information through the senses

- **Cross-lateral integration** (cross-crawl): coordinating both sides of the brain through body movement

- **Memory:** retaining and retrieving information

A Brief Glossary of Brain Terms

Axons: fibers that send impulses from one neuron to another

Basal ganglia: deeply placed masses of gray matter within each cerebral hemisphere

Cerebrum: area of the brain that monitors thinking, memory, and speech

Cerebellum: area of the brain that controls coordination, movement, and muscle use

Dendrites: fibers that receive impulses from neurons

Frontal lobes: the anterior division of each cerebral hemisphere

Limbic system: area of the brain that controls the emotions and motivation

Neurons: the nerve cells of the brain

Synapses: the tiny spaces between the axons and dendrites in different neurons

Language Boosters

Children process language in the frontal lobe of the brain's left hemisphere. They process verbal information into receptive and expressive vocabulary. The left brain is the area where information is organized, sequenced, and analyzed. Combining these skills with the creativity of the brain's right hemisphere creates a balanced approach to developing essential skills for communication, reading, and writing.

Talk About It

BRAINWAVE Emotions are sometimes difficult for young children to talk about, particularly if those emotions are their own! Use pictures to spark a discussion about feelings. In the process, children will use the parts of their brain that express the language of emotions, enabling them to empathize with others.

HOW TO

1. Ask children how they are feeling today. You will probably get an answer like "good!" or "bad!" Most children need to practice using words for different emotions. Model different words by telling how you are feeling that day. *I feel zippy* (or *sad* or *excited*). You can do this every day at meeting time.

2. Show an evocative picture. Ask, *What might be happening? How does the person in this picture feel?* Suggest that children make up a story about the picture.

3. Encourage children to suggest different emotion words to describe the situation in the picture. Write their ideas on chart paper.

4. Invite children to imagine what might happen next. *How will the person feel? How would you feel? How would you like the story to end?*

SKILLS

Observing
Comparing
Expressive and receptive language
Other Skills:
Empathy

MATERIALS

- pictures of people pasted on cardboard (taken from drawings, magazine photos, even comics), chart paper, marker

CHANGE THE VARIABLE

- Read a story aloud only part of the way through. Stop and ask children to share how they think the character is feeling. Read on and compare the emotions at the end of the story with those at the middle.

What's Next?

BRAINWAVE Sequencing—the ability to organize events into a pattern—is essential to expressive language development. It is very hard for a child to communicate an idea if he or she cannot organize thoughts into an understandable sequence. This skill is also used in reading, since the process of interpreting a line of text involves the ability to recognize the pattern and sequence of letters and words. By providing children with many concrete opportunities to experiment with and create sequences, you help them utilize the part of the brain that governs these skills.

HOW TO

1. Show a set of pictures and invite children to talk about what they see in each. *What do you see in the pictures? What is happening in each? Has anything changed from one picture to the next?*

2. Invite children to find the sequence in the pictures and arrange them in order. *If this was a story, what might happen first? Which picture shows what happens next? Which picture shows the end of the story?*

3. Encourage children to tell the story of the pictures. *What might happen next? If there was a fourth picture for this story, what would it show?* Continue the story to see if their predictions were accurate.

4. Suggest mixing up the cards and retelling the story a new way.

SKILLS

Sequencing
Inferring
Deducing
Expressive and receptive
   language

MATERIALS

- sets of pictures or photos mounted on cardboard that show a beginning, a middle, and an end (cut from magazines, comics, or old picture books)

- photos of children in class-room routines or events

CHANGE THE VARIABLE

- Put sequence cards in the literacy center for children to experiment with. Invite them to mix and match different pictures to create more and more stories. They might tape-record themselves telling the story for others to listen to while matching the sequence cards.

- Play a "what's missing?" game. Lay out two cards from a sequence and invite children to guess what part of the story is missing.

Guess Who?

BRAINWAVE. Children develop language skills through wordplay. Riddles are excellent brain builders: They require children to make connections, inferences, and deductions. Not only is the process of answering riddles important—so is the creating of clues. This activity invites children to do both!

HOW TO

1. Secretly choose one child per week for this activity. Invite him or her to bring in several baby pictures from home.

2. Together with the child, place each picture in a photo album sleeve. Suggest that the child make up clues about him- or herself. Ask questions to solicit answers to be used as clues: *What do you look like now? What do you like to do? What can you do now that you could not do when you were little? How many brothers and sisters do you have? What pets do you have?*

3. Write the clues on index cards and attach them to posterboard. Also attach the baby pictures.

4. Invite the group to look at the pictures and read the clues with you. Ask, *Who could the mystery child be?* Leave the pictures and clues up for a week so that children have time to examine and discuss them. Children can vote for whom they think it is as you record their guesses on chart paper.

5. At the end of the week, have the child reveal himself or herself!

I have curly hair

I like to swim

I have two brothers

I have a cat

I live in an apartment

I have freckles

SKILLS

Inferring
Deducing
Expressive and receptive language
Problem solving

MATERIALS

○ children's baby pictures, 3- by 5 index cards, magnetic photo album pages, posterboard, marker

CHANGE THE VARIABLE

❂ Make up simple riddles for a hidden object in a bag and invite children to guess what it is, based on the clues.

❂ Send home paper lunch bags and ask children to bring in an object from home for the class to use in a riddle game. Help them make up clues by asking, *What color (shape, size) is it? How do you use it? What can you do with it?*

Who's Missing?

BRAINWAVE. The brain can store an amazing amount of information. By playing *memory games*, children make connections in their neural pathways, strengthening their ability to store, retrieve, and use information.

HOW TO

 Invite one child to be the guesser. While he turns around and hides his eyes, ask another child to volunteer to hide under the sheet. (It is helpful to have the hiding child stay in the place where he or she was sitting. This provides an extra clue for the guesser!)

(2) Say, *Abracadabra, open your eyes, who has disappeared before your eyes?* If the guesser has trouble, invite the others to give clues describing the missing person. They might say whether it is a boy or a girl, or tell what the hair color or favorite activity of the person is.

(3) When the guesser guesses correctly, the hiding child can be the next guesser!

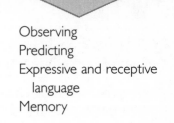

SKILLS

Observing
Predicting
Expressive and receptive
    language
Memory

MATERIALS

⚙ an old bedsheet

CHANGE THE VARIABLE

@ Place a few interesting items on a tray for children to see, then cover the tray with a cloth while you remove something. Show the tray again and ask what's missing. (Make it more complicated by rearranging the items on the tray as well as removing one. Or, try removing more than one item!)

Backwards Day

BRAINWAVE. What would happen if children came to school and many of their familiar materials were upside down? What if you started the day with a closing circle and worked backwards? You would be providing the brain with novelty. The brain loves to wonder and question. Unusual things and events invite the brain to pay attention!

HOW TO

1. Prepare the room before children arrive. Greet them at the door with a hearty "Goodbye!" Walk around the room backwards.

2. Go through the day in reverse order, starting with your ending activity. You might also:

   Place drawing paper under the surface of the table in the art corner and invite children to work upside down.

   Construct a block building for children to take down and then build up!

   Have children put their heads between their legs and look at the room from upside down. What is different? How does it feel? Have them suggest other things they could do backwards or upside down.

3. Invite children to point out all the upside-down and backwards things they see throughout the day!

SKILLS

Problem solving
Creative thinking
Expressive and receptive
   language
Observing
Predicting

MATERIALS

✿ the entire classroom turned upside down and backwards: put some chairs and tables upside down, turn posters and books on the bookshelf upside down, wear a pin or your glasses upside down, and so on

CHANGE THE VARIABLE

@ Have children line up by walking backwards (carefully!).

@ Write and say children's first names backwards for the day.

@ Try to read a book at story time upside down or backwards!

13 @

Silly Silly Bo Billy

BRAINWAVE. Humor is an important part of healthy brain development. Laughter actually affects the balance of chemicals in the brain! Laughter releases seratonin in the brain, affecting stress levels and the mind's ability to process new information.

HOW TO

1. Use the old '60s song "The Name Game" to create a silly song for each child. Use your own name to show how the song works. Invite children to clap along as you sing it. For instance: *Ellen, Ellen, bo bellen, banana fana fo fellen, fe fi mo mellen, Ellen!* It is helpful to write the chant on a chart for children to see the pattern of the letter changes in front of the name in the song.

2. Invite a child to offer his or her name for the song. For example: *Jerry, Jerry bo berry, banana fana fo ferry, fe fi mo merry, Jerry!*

3. Write each child's chant on drawing paper, leaving space for each child to illustrate it with a self-portrait.

4. Put it all together into a class Silly Name Book!

SKILLS

Expressive and receptive language
Creative thinking
Other Skills:
Phonemic awareness

MATERIALS

- chart paper, drawing paper, crayons and markers

CHANGE THE VARIABLE

- Create silly versions of nursery rhymes using the names of children in the class. For instance, for "Mary, Mary, Quite Contrary," invite children to suggest the silly things they would like to grow in their garden. The rhyme can become: "Frankie, Frankie, Frankie Jones, How does your garden grow? With meatballs and spaghetti and lots of trucks in a row!"

The Rhyming Box

BRAINWAVE

Rhyming is another way the brain makes connections between the sound of words and syllables. Some young children grasp rhyming quickly, while the concept is elusive to others. You can make the rhyming process visual and experiential for children by having them match real objects that rhyme.

HOW TO

1. Share the box and its contents with the group. Invite children to name and discuss the objects. *Do you notice anything about the names of these objects?* Demonstrate one rhyming pair by showing the objects and saying their rhyming names.

2. Ask one child to close his or her eyes, take something from the box, open his or her eyes, and say its name.

3. Have the child look in the box to find the matching rhyming object.

4. The box is passed to other players until it is empty.

5. You might extend the rhyming experience by inviting children to use the items in the box to tell a rhyming story! ("Once upon a time the bear in the chair found a sock with a rock in it . . .")

SKILLS

Creative thinking
Expressive and receptive language
Matching
Sensory-motor
Other Skills:
Auditory discrimination
Phonemic awareness

MATERIALS

* a large shoe box with a lid, a collection of small objects whose names make rhyming pairs (cork and fork, bell and shell, toy bear and toy chair, small chain and toy train, toy duck and toy truck, toy bed and toy sled, sock and rock)

CHANGE THE VARIABLE

* Ask children to look around the room for two small items that rhyme, then add them to the box.

ABC Clothesline

BRAINWAVE. Matching real objects to an abstract concept or symbol is one way the brain makes meaning. When children see how things fit together in an orderly pattern, they can better understand the information the brain is receiving through the senses of touch, sight, and sound.

HOW TO

1. Hang a clothesline low along one wall. Children can help you attach the clothespins (mounted with letter cards) in alphabetical order along the line.

2. Ask, *What can we hang on the clothespins? Can you find pictures that start with the same letter as a card on the alphabet line?* Have children match the objects with the letters and hang them up.

3. After the line is full, invite children to select different pictures to use in telling a story. They can take turns removing a picture from the line and use it as a prompt or prop for the story. Record the collaborative story on chart paper!

SKILLS

Matching
Sequencing
Other Skills:
Auditory discrimination
Phonemic awareness
Letter recognition

MATERIALS

○ length of rope or clothesline, clothespins, letter cards, a collection of pictures (cut from magazines) representing the letters A to Z (apple, ball, candy, and so on), chart paper, markers

CHANGE THE VARIABLE

◎ Reverse the process and go on a letter treasure hunt. Write the letters of the alphabet on three- by five-inch cards. Give several to each child and invite everyone to hunt for an object in the room that starts with that letter.

The Brainy Box

BRAINWAVE. Many teachers have used a "feely box" in their classrooms at one time or another. The process of matching the sensory experience of the object with the visual is an important part of brain development. Children use all of their senses when they interact with new information—just watch a baby put everything in her mouth! When you focus children's attention on the sense of touch, you not only help them make synaptic connections, but you engage them in making predictions and testing hypotheses.

HOW TO

1. Place a collection of objects in the pillowcase. Spread out the matching cards on the table or floor next to the pillowcase and invite a child to reach inside and find an object to feel. Ask him or her to use the other hand to touch or point to the picture of the object. Then the child can take it out of the pillowcase to see if they match!

2. Play it in reverse. Ask a child to choose a picture card first and then find the matching object.

3. Do it a different way! This time, put in objects that make a sound (a rattle, keys, a bell, a maraca, and so on). *Can you match the object to a picture outside the pillowcase?*

SKILLS

Sensory-motor
Observing
Predicting
Expressive and receptive
  language
Matching
Other Skills:
Fine motor coordination

MATERIALS

○ pillowcase, small objects of different textures and shapes, pictures or drawings that correspond to objects in the pillowcase (for instance, if you have an apple in the pillowcase, have a card with a picture of an apple on it)

CHANGE THE VARIABLE

◒ Play a "feel and say" game. In this version, children use descriptive language to tell about what they are feeling in the bag. Other children guess what it is based on the description.

Fun With the Five Senses

BRAINWAVE. Sensory experience stimulates brain development.
Children perceive the world through their
senses, and are often surprised by how many ways they use their senses in
everyday activities!

HOW TO

1. Show the body-part pictures as you introduce the concept of the five senses. Ask, *What do you use your ears for? eyes? mouth? nose? hands and feet?*

2. Have children pantomime common activities such as eating, drinking, walking, riding a bike, and so on. Ask children what body parts and senses you use to do these things.

3. Now take the concrete experience to the level of abstraction. Use pictures representing everyday activities. Show a picture and ask, *What senses would you use if you were playing a drum like the child in this picture? How many different senses would you use?* Repeat with another picture.

4. Reverse the game and use the body-part pictures as charades clues. One at a time, have each child draw a card and, without showing it to anyone, act out an activity that someone might do with that sense. For example, for the mouth/taste card, a child might pretend to lick a lollipop or eat a sandwich. The child pantomimes different actions until the others guess the sense!

SKILLS

Sensory-motor
Expressive language
Problem solving

MATERIALS

- pictures depicting familiar activities (cut from magazines or old books), one picture for each of the body parts used in the five senses: eye, ear, mouth, hand, nose

CHANGE THE VARIABLE

- *How would you use your five senses to describe an apple? a banana? a block?* Expand children's descriptive language skills by inviting them to explore an object with their five senses. Allow children to manipulate the object and invite them to describe what they see, hear, smell, feel, and taste.

Arts Boosters

The arts influence and shape healthy development of all parts of the brain, and in turn, these parts of the brain mediate creativity. While practicing the arts is usually thought of as a right-brain activity, the left brain is involved in figuring out how to express or create. Music has a strong math component, and art can be concrete and even linear! Music influences the function of the midbrain, dance and artful play influence the limbic region, and drama, storytelling, and writing influences the cortical region. Try these activities to engage both hemispheres of the brain in the arts. Children will enjoy the open-ended nature of these activities that support their creative processes.

Here I Am

BRAINWAVE.

Did you know that art is an excellent activity for developing problem-solving skills? Give a child a challenge, and his or her brain will become engaged and attentive. Allow children choices of methods and materials, and you have the perfect recipe for creating motivation and focus—key ingredients for learning success!

HOW TO

1. Invite children to look into their hand mirrors. Ask, *What words would you use to describe yourself?*

2. Show children how to make a shadow with a flashlight. Have children take turns getting their silhouettes traced onto butcher paper.

3. Invite children to draw their features on their silhouette and add yarn hair.

4. Suggest that children fill their silhouettes with drawings, photos, stickers, collage items, or anything else that represents the child. Ask children to think about things they like, such as their favorite color, food, hobbies, and so on. They can draw and paste these on the picture, too! The goal is to fill up the space of the silhouette with "me" things.

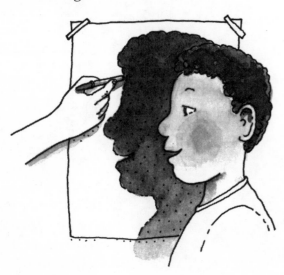

✦ SKILLS ✦

Creative thinking
Problem solving
Other Skills:
Fine motor coordination

❂ MATERIALS ❂

✿ flashlight, large sheets of butcher paper (one per child), markers or crayons, a variety of collage and art materials, yarn, glue, unbreakable hand mirrors

CHANGE THE VARIABLE

❧ Make an As We See Ourselves class book. Take photos of children with a disposable camera. Paste these on one page and have children draw their self-portrait on the other. Encourage children to write or dictate anything they want to say about themselves, too!

Box Museum

BRAINWAVE. We can't prepare children for the specific problems they will encounter in the future but we can help them develop the problem-solving skills they will need to handle them. Here is an artistic and fun way to do just that!

HOW TO

1. Strategically place several boxes of different sizes and shapes in the art area. Ask, *What could we do with these boxes? If you were an inventor, what would you make from these boxes?* Allow children plenty of time to brainstorm different ideas, writing them down on chart paper.

2. Show children where to find the materials they can use with their inventions, and stand back to watch the master artists/inventors at work.

3. Allow children opportunities to deal independently with any problems they encounter as they try to put boxes and materials together.

4. If children ask for help, ask questions to take them to the next level of thinking instead of fixing it for them: *What do you want to do? What materials do we have that can make this work?* You might need to demonstrate, but then stand back again.

5. Create a "box museum" to show off children's inventions!

SKILLS

Creative thinking
Problem solving
Flexible thinking
Other Skills:
Fine motor coordination

MATERIALS

- empty cardboard boxes in a variety of shapes and sizes, paper plates, a collection of "junk materials" (Styrofoam, plastic lids, game pieces and manipulatives, buttons, yarn, fabric and paper scraps, brass fasteners, pipe cleaners, bread ties), chart paper, markers, glue

CHANGE THE VARIABLE

- Try using blocks instead of boxes, but limit the type. What can children do with only square blocks, triangles, or arches?

Paint Possibilities

BRAINWAVE Having choices of methods and materials empowers children and supports emotional growth. In this activity, children experiment with a familiar medium—paint.

HOW TO

1. Invite children to examine the different types of paper you have collected. *What do you notice about these? How are they the same or different? Can we paint on these? How many different kinds of paper can we paint on? Will the paint stick to all of them? Let's see!*

2. Put different painting surfaces in different areas of the room. Encourage children to try each of the surfaces.

3. Have a "sidewalk art show" of children's works. Don't forget to ask them to title their masterpieces!

SKILLS

Creative thinking
Problem solving
Flexible thinking

MATERIALS

❂ an assortment of tempera paint colors, paintbrushes in different sizes, different types of paper (posterboard, easel paper, fingerpaint paper, newspaper, egg cartons, adding-machine tape, wallpaper, sandpaper, paper plates, freezer and corrugated paper), newspaper or dropcloths

CHANGE THE VARIABLE

❧ Change the tools children paint with! Try a sponge, a feather, marbles, a pine bough, and so on.

❧ Change the paint! Try everything from fingerpaint to watercolors, or add glitter to tempera paint!

Grab a Bag of Art!

BRAINWAVE.

Art is a process—artists experiment with materials and techniques in creating new works. The creative arts activate the cortical and limbic areas of the brain. Here is a simple way to improvise with art and scrap materials!

HOW TO

1. Put different recyclable art and scrap materials in paper lunch bags, making sure that no bags have exactly the same contents. Include one item (such as a paper plate or small cardboard sheet) in each bag that can be used as a base for the child's creation.

2. Ask children to choose a "grab bag"—just like at a party! To avoid conflict, define each individual space for children to empty the contents (you might use a piece of construction paper or styrofoam tray per child).

3. Ask, *What can you do with the things in your bag? How do you want to put them together?* Encourage children to explore different ways to use the materials before they choose one way to finish their creation.

4. Invite children to create signs from index cards and display their work.

SKILLS

Creative thinking
Problem solving
Flexible thinking

MATERIALS

- paper plates, cardboard squares, construction paper, a variety of scrap and art materials, brown paper lunch bags (one per child), glue, tape, brass fasteners, pipe cleaners, crayons, paints, markers, index cards

CHANGE THE VARIABLE

- Change the contents of the bags to all wood, all paper, or all fabric items. *What can you make with these?*

- Change the task. Instead of an art piece, have children use the materials to make an instrument!

Scene-Setting Sheets

BRAINWAVE. Imitating and pretending are an important part of early childhood development. They provide opportunities to try on different roles, to problem-solve, and to express emotions. Open-ended dramatic play and movement are core curricula for the brain!

HOW TO

1. Show the pillowcase to children and say, *I brought this bag to school today for a fun project, but now I can't remember what to do with it. Can you help me?*

2. Have children help you take the sheets out of the pillow-case and invite them to brainstorm all the different things that might be done with them. *How many ways can we use these around the room? How could we use them in the block area? the dramatic play area? the playground?*

3. Write their ideas on chart paper.

4. After children have brainstormed ideas, it's time to try some of them out! During activity times, have children use the sheets in different areas of the room, starting with the dramatic play area. If possible, videotape their work to show them later!

SKILLS

Problem solving
Creative thinking
Perceptual-motor
Other Skills:
Creative dramatics and movement

MATERIALS

- several old bedsheets or yards of fabric stuffed into a large pillowcase, chart paper, markers

CHANGE THE VARIABLE

- Suggest a new dimension by adding scarves and smaller strips of fabric to the dramatic play.

- Play a variety of music. *How can you use the sheets to move to the music?*

- Take the sheets and scarves outside and have children create environments there.

Pass the Rhythm Pattern

BRAINWAVE The brain attends to both patterns and novelty. Experiences with musical patterns deepen the experience because they are multisensory.

HOW TO

1) "Pass" a rhythm pattern around the group. Start a beat, such as 1-2-3, 1-2-3 and then "pass" it to the child next to you, who repeats the pattern and passes it to the next child, and so on. Keep children interested by changing the beat or increasing the speed!

2) Now, move to the next level of abstraction by playing a rhythmic guessing game. Clap the pattern of a familiar song and see if children can guess what it is (use familiar songs such as "The Farmer in the Dell" or "Twinkle, Twinkle Little Star"). Reinforce their answer while adding the verbal dimension by singing it together.

3) Add the visual dimension by creating picture patterns for children to "read" and clap. You can draw or paste pictures of vehicles (such as: car-car-tractor, car-car-tractor) for children to read, say, and clap.

SKILLS

Sensory-motor
Matching
Patterning
Creative thinking

MATERIALS

- rhythm sticks (one pair per child), small drums, chart paper, markers

CHANGE THE VARIABLE

- Add other instruments to the pattern making, or alternate the volume!

Sound Play

BRAINWAVE. Music activities can help develop language and math skills. Research suggests that music helps promote the development of brain regions involved in many different cognitive tasks. Add creative thinking and problem solving, and the result is a fully engaged (and interested) child.

HOW TO

1. Sing a favorite song together. *What if we wanted to add some instruments to accompany our singing? What could we find to make sounds?*

2. Send children on a "treasure hunt" around the room looking for objects that can make a sound or help keep a beat. Reconvene for a demonstration of their finds.

3. Encourage children to explore all the different sounds their "instrument" can make. Sing the song again, adding the dimension of the new classroom band instruments.

4. Change the words to the marching song "When the Saints Go Marching In" to "When the BAND Goes Marching In" and have a parade of instruments! You might even tape children's "songs"!

SKILLS

Problem solving
Observing
Comparing
Creative thinking

MATERIALS

- anything that makes a sound (pencils, rulers, blocks, sandbox tools, spoons, keys, beaters, bells, pots and pans, plastic containers)
  optional: tape or video-recorder

CHANGE THE VARIABLE

- Take it outside! *Can you make an instrument with nature objects?*

- Have children bring in something from home to use as an instrument.

Musical Sound Effects

BRAINWAVE. Listening and matching are important elements in the development of math and reading abilities. Focusing is not an easy task for young children, but if the activity is new and different, the child is more likely to attend to the task. Add the context of a story, and the essential component of motivation is there. In this activity, matching sounds to words enhances children's ability to problem-solve.

HOW TO

1. Read a familiar tale. Ask, *What were some of the characters or events in the story?* Don't worry if children remember things in story sequence; just record their ideas as they say them.

2. Show the different instruments and invite children to consider how they could be used to add sound effects to the story (for instance, drums for thunder, bells every time a certain character is mentioned). Record their choices on chart paper.

3. Have children choose instruments and read the story again, asking them to play their instruments when appropriate. Remind children they will have to listen very carefully for their part of the story.

SKILLS

Observing
Comparing
Matching
Creative thinking
Other Skills:
Auditory discrimination
Listening

MATERIALS

○ rhythm instruments, a familiar repetitive story such as "The Gingerbread Man," "Three Billy Goats Gruff" or "The House That Jack Built"

CHANGE THE VARIABLE

○ Add sound effects to familiar repetitive songs such as "The Wheels on the Bus" or "I Know an Old Lady" or "This Old Man."

○ Tape-record the story and put it with the instruments in the listening corner for children to use independently.

Are You My Brother?

BRAINWAVE. Sensory experiences enhance synaptic growth. What happens when you eliminate one sense and rely more on another? The brain gathers and uses the experiential information and makes new connections. In this activity, children take away the sense of sight to heighten their sense of sound.

HOW TO

1 Talk about getting lost. *Have you ever been lost in a crowd? How did you find your family? Did you see or hear them first?*

2 Find a large area in which to move without obstacles. Explain that the object of the game is to use your sense of hearing to find someone who is making the same sound as you (that person is your "brother" or "sister").

3 Play the game first with children keeping their eyes open. Whisper the name of an animal to each child in the group (four children per animal). Use familiar animals with distinctive sounds, such as a cat, dog, lion, or snake. Then have children spread out into the movement space and slowly move around, making their animal sound. When children find a matching animal sound, they hold hands and go looking for the others in their group.

4 The next time, have children close their eyes and CAREFULLY move around the space listening for the matching sounds. When they find a match they can sit down together and continue making their sound until all the children have found their group!

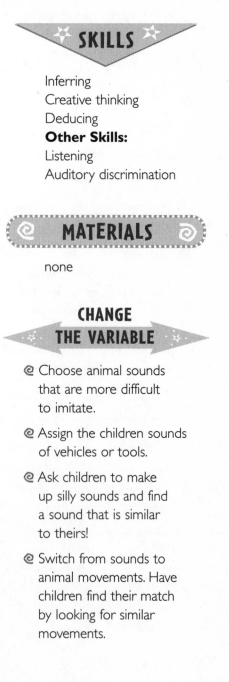

SKILLS

Inferring
Creative thinking
Deducing
Other Skills:
Listening
Auditory discrimination

MATERIALS

CHANGE THE VARIABLE

- Choose animal sounds that are more difficult to imitate.

- Assign the children sounds of vehicles or tools.

- Ask children to make up silly sounds and find a sound that is similar to theirs!

- Switch from sounds to animal movements. Have children find their match by looking for similar movements.

The Power of Four

BRAINWAVE Some research shows that a child's thinking may be enhanced by listening to music with a strong rhythmic pattern of four beats. This predictable pattern, found often in the works of great composers such as Mozart, Bach, and Handel, might provide sensory input that is both comforting and supportive of thinking and problem solving.

HOW TO

1. Play the music and encourage children to move their arms to the beat while sitting in place.

2. Next, invite them to stand and move. *How can you make low movements without leaving your place? How can you make high movements? Can you make movements to the music somewhere in the middle?*

3. Change to a different composer and ask children to move freely around the room to the 4-4 beat. *Can you count the beat as you move?*

4. Gather children together in a circle and ask them to walk around the circle clapping and stepping on the beat: 1-2-3-4, 1-2-3-4, and so on.

 **SKILLS**

Patterning
Problem solving
Sequencing
Other Skills:
Listening
Counting

MATERIALS

○ recorded music by Mozart, Handel, or Bach

CHANGE THE VARIABLE

● Play popular music with a similar 1-2-3-4 beat. *How is it the same or different?*

● Have children move to music with a different beat, such as 1-2-3, 1-2-3, 1-2-3. *How does that feel different? How does it make you want to move?*

Physical Boosters

How is the young child's brain involved in the development of physical skills? Children learn by doing! Using small and large muscles not only strengthens the body but engages specific areas of the brain. The cortex, cerebellum, and basal ganglia mediate physical coordination and govern body movement and equilibrium. With these activities, you can engage children through opportunities to problem-solve with their body.

The Cross-Crawl Obstacle Course

BRAINWAVE You've heard about the two hemispheres of the brain: the right and the left, each of which controls different functions. When a physical activity requires the movement to cross over the midline of the body, the two sides must work together, thus engaging the whole child. These skills are actually prerequisites for the development of eye-hand coordination and visual-perceptual motor tasks, such as reading!

HOW TO

1. Ask children to crawl (choose a safe, open space). Remind them to move opposite hands and feet when they crawl. (Crawling is one of the first midline-crossing activities babies learn. It is always helpful for older children to go back to those skills and practice.)

2. Create an obstacle course with things for children to crawl in and out of, over and under, up and down. Include activities that invite them to move their hands or feet over the midline, such as crawling through a horizontal ladder or a row of tires.

3. Put on some fun movement music and let the crawling begin! You might hang a low curtain or sheet over some of the objects so children have to stay low in their crawl.

4. Invite children to pretend they are alligators or crocodiles as they crawl through the course!

SKILLS

Perceptual-motor
Cross-lateral integration
Problem solving
Other Skills:
Gross motor coordination
Fine motor coordination

MATERIALS

 old bedsheets, chalk, hula hoops, tires, ladder, blocks, or any other material that can be used to create an obstacle course

CHANGE THE VARIABLE

- Invite children to start at the opposite end of the course.

- Suggest that children do the course backwards.

Back-to-Back Necklaces

BRAINWAVE Have you ever found yourself wiggling or tapping your fingers while thinking? Fidgeting may not be all bad! Research has found that finger movements and manipulation of small objects actually promotes brain development.

HOW TO

1 Have children pair off. Put out two sets of beads and strings for each pair and invite children to freely string the beads and objects, then remove the beads or objects from the string.

2 Show children how to sit back-to-back, so that they cannot see what their partner is doing. Let them choose who is to be the leader of the pair first. That child starts by describing the bead he or she is putting on the string, such as, "I am putting on a big red bead." The other child listens (without looking) and puts a bead that fits the description on his or her string.

3 Then the leader describes the next bead he or she wishes to add, such as, "Next is a small blue bead." This process continues until the string is filled.

4 At the end, each pair turns around and compares strings. *How are your strings the same or different?* Talk about whether it was easy or hard to follow directions.

5 Have children trade roles and repeat the activity.

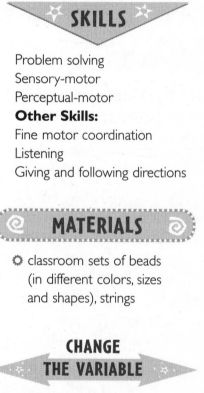

✧ SKILLS ✧

Problem solving
Sensory-motor
Perceptual-motor
Other Skills:
Fine motor coordination
Listening
Giving and following directions

MATERIALS

○ classroom sets of beads (in different colors, sizes and shapes), strings

CHANGE THE VARIABLE

☙ Play follow-the-leader at the easel, with one child describing the lines and shapes she or he is painting or drawing, while the other listens and tries to come up with the same!

☙ Play back-to-back block building, using similar piles of blocks for each child.

Web Weaving

BRAINWAVE

The brain's two hemispheres (the right and the left) each have specific functions. The left is more analytic and logical and the right is more intuitive and spontaneous. Combining fine motor manipulation with problem solving and group process in this activity engages the whole child—and both hemispheres of the brain.

HOW TO

1. Warm children up by singing "The Itsy Bitsy Spider" together (using the finger movements).

2. Talk about spider webs. *Have you ever seen a web? What did it look like?*

3. Show children the string and suggest the idea of making a web of children. *How could we use this rope to make a giant web of all of us?* Encourage children to brainstorm suggestions.

4. Put on the musical accompaniment and start weaving! **Weave yourself first in order to demonstrate a safe way to wrap the rope around the waist without tying a knot or wrapping it too tightly.**

5. Roll the ball of rope to a child across the circle and ask that he or she wraps him- or herself in it. He or she then rolls the ball to another child to do the same, until all children are "woven in."

6. Ask, *How can we move while we are all connected?* Invite children to stand slowly and move around the circle to the music. Children have to cooperate to be able to move as one!

SKILLS

Problem solving
Determining cause and effect
Other Skills:
Cooperation
Fine motor coordination
Gross motor coordination

MATERIALS

○ large ball of thick, soft, smooth string or yarn, musical accompaniment such as Mozart, Bach or Purcell

CHANGE THE VARIABLE

❂ Cooperation skills are also needed for the group to figure out a way to unravel itself at the end of the activity. Children can reverse the process or simply step out of the rope!

Mini-Movements

BRAINWAVE. Fidget those digits! Movements of the fingers activate cognitive development in young children. Creative activities using fine motor skills have also been found to assist maltreated children.

HOW TO

1) Roll out the paper on the floor and tape it in place. Invite children to find a place alongside the paper where they can lay on their stomachs to paint. Put out several colors of fingerpaint and put on music.

2) Encourage children to make a variety of tiny movements with their fingers as they fingerpaint. *Can you make tiny circles or figure eights? Can you use the fingers on both hands at once? Can you cross one hand over the other and paint with your fingers that way?*

3) Change the music and invite children to try other finger movements that the new music inspires. *Can you tap your fingers in the paint? Can you make your fingers leap off the paper?*

4) Hang the finished art piece in the hall for all to see!

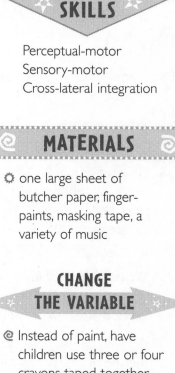

SKILLS

Perceptual-motor
Sensory-motor
Cross-lateral integration

MATERIALS

⚙ one large sheet of butcher paper, finger-paints, masking tape, a variety of music

CHANGE THE VARIABLE

🌀 Instead of paint, have children use three or four crayons taped together. *Can you make big motions and little motions? How are they different?*

Getting From Here to There

BRAINWAVE.

Problem solving takes on a new dimension when it is applied to a gross motor activity. It provides exercise for both the muscles and the brain. It has been found that physical activity helps the brain to better process and retain information. How many times have you gone for a walk to "clear your head"?

HOW TO

1) Place two strips of masking tape on the floor, parallel to each other and as far apart as possible. Explain that the lines show where to start and where to go in the game.

2) Have children all sit on one line. Put on some music and invite children to move. *How can you move over to the other line without taking your bottom off the floor? Try it!* Children may choose to wiggle, slide, or scoot. When everyone is on the other line, have them describe what they did.

3) Next, have children use flexible thinking by going back to the other line, moving in a different way! *How can you move back differently, still keeping your bottom on the floor?*

4) Keep changing the instructions for children's movements back and forth. They can try moving on their tummies, knees, feet, or backwards!

SKILLS

Perceptual-motor
Problem solving
Flexible thinking
Other Skills:
Gross motor coordination
Cooperation

MATERIALS

✿ masking tape, music

CHANGE THE VARIABLE

@ Invite children to pretend to be certain types of animals as they move across the floor.

@ Have children move with a partner. *How many ways can you move together?*

The Cross-Crawl Limbo

BRAINWAVE Have you ever done the limbo? The trick is to get yourself low enough to move under a pole without knocking it off its supports, a task that involves important gross-motor and problem-solving skills. Children will use the cross-crawl movement, which requires coordination of the two hemispheres of the brain.

HOW TO

1. Put on music and invite children to move freely to get warmed up.

2. Show children the pole, explaining that they are going to play a traditional game from the Caribbean. Have two volunteers lightly hold the stick at a comfortable height (about waist-high).

3. Ask children to line up on one side and find a way to go under the stick without bumping it. Each time through, lower the stick a bit. Children will have to find a new way to get low and go under. Eventually, they will have to crawl forward on their stomachs to dip beneath the pole.

4. To end the game, invite children to try it one more time, this time crawling backwards.

SKILLS

Cross-lateral integration
Perceptual-motor
Problem solving
Other Skills:
Cooperation
Gross motor coordination

MATERIALS

○ broom or lightweight pole, lively music

CHANGE THE VARIABLE

℮ Reverse the game. Start with the stick low and invite children to find different ways to go over it!

Keep Your Balance

BRAINWAVE Balance is an important part of physical development. Laterality (the awareness and coordination of the two sides of the body) and directionality (the ability to see where something is coming from, or to see its placement in space) are strengthened by balance activities. These skills are core to reading and writing.

HOW TO

 Ask children to balance on one foot, then the other. *On which foot is it easier to balance?* Then ask them to balance on one foot and cross their arms (which requires them to cross the midline of the body). *Is it easier or harder to balance with your arms crossed?*

 Next, have them try balancing and moving. Put down a line of masking tape on the floor and encourage children to walk across it without stepping off. Notice which foot they lead with as they walk.

③ Have them try it again, leading with the other foot. *Can you walk backwards on the line without stepping off? Can you walk across with your arms folded?*

④ Suggest they try different ways of walking (forwards, backwards, sideways, on tiptoe, hopping, and so on), along the line.

SKILLS

Perceptual-motor
Creative thinking
Other Skills:
Gross motor coordination
Laterality
Directionality

MATERIALS

⚙ masking tape

CHANGE THE VARIABLE

◉ Add a prop. *Can you walk the line balancing a bean bag on your head? Or while you're bouncing a ball? Can two of you balance a ball between you and walk the line?*

◉ Graduate to a real balance beam or a low curb. Try some of the challenges again, adding the dimension of height.

37

What a Racquet!

BRAINWAVE. Eye-hand coordination is the skill of using the eyes and hands (or feet) together, with the eyes informing the hands where or how to move. Through practice, the brain helps the body develop the capacity to successfully complete these tasks. Here's a fun way to practice!

HOW TO

1. Help children make simple racquets. Stretch open the wire hangers so that they form an open diamond shape, with the hooks bent in at the bottom. Then have children open their stockings and stretch them over the frames, creating racquets.

2. Help children tape the stockings in place and wrap tape over the hook end to form a handle.

3. Now you are ready to play! Set up two children with one ball or birdie and ask them to slowly and gently tap it back and forth. Start them out close together and then have them move farther and farther apart.

4. Invite children to play in small groups.

SKILLS

Cross-lateral integration
Other Skills:
Eye-hand coordination
Gross motor coordination
Cooperation

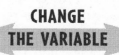
MATERIALS

○ wire coat hangers (cover the sharp ends with masking tape), old stockings or panty hose, pliers, sturdy tape, and small, lightweight balls (such as soft foam balls or a badminton birdie).

CHANGE THE VARIABLE

◉ If children want to play alone, they can hit their balls against a wall.

◉ Make a bowling game. Place a small amount of sand in the bottom of empty plastic soda bottles, and tape the tops closed. Then have children roll a ball to knock 'em down!

Dance-a-Graph

BRAINWAVE

When school math activities are experienced kinesthetically and concretely, children develop a deeper understanding of the concept being taught. In this activity, children experience "being" the items in a graph!

HOW TO

1. Place two lines of masking tape on the floor, perpendicular from a free wall space in an open area.

2. Put the "boy" picture card at the start of one line and the "girl" at the start of the other.

3. Explain that the game is like musical chairs. When the music plays, children can dance freely, but when the music stops, boys should stand on the line with the boy picture, and girls should go to the other. Put on the dance music and have them start.

4. Stop the music and let children find their places. Invite them to compare how many people are in each line. *Which line has the most? the least? Reach across and hold the hand of someone across from you in the other line. Does everyone have a hand to hold? Why or why not?*

5. Put the music on again for children to dance to. While they are moving, change the pictures above the lines to a different category, such as hair color or eye color.

SKILLS

Classifying
Deducing
Perceptual-motor
Other Skills:
Graphing
Gross motor coordination

MATERIALS

- picture cards (to mark the different categories to be graphed) with simple drawings of boy/girl, light eyes/dark eyes, long hair/short hair, masking tape, music

CHANGE THE VARIABLE

- Ask, *Can you move like an animal? a vehicle?* Put up pictures representing land, water, and air over three different lines. *Where does your animal or vehicle line up?*

Turtle Crawl

BRAINWAVE Activities that combine a number of tasks at once challenge the brain. Using multiple parts of the brain in a single action helps promote healthy brain development. Here, children will cross the midline, coordinate right and left hemispheres, and solve a problem—all in one activity.

HOW TO

1 Discuss turtles. *What do you know about turtles? What do they look like? How do they move?* Write children's thoughts on chart paper.

2 Challenge children to crawl like turtles around an open space. *What is on a turtle's back? Can you pretend to be a turtle using this towel as your shell? How can you crawl around without losing it?*

3 Put on some music and watch children figure out how to crawl with a "shell" on their back.

4 Give children a destination and challenge them to get from one place to another without their shell coming off!

SKILLS

Cross-lateral integration
Problem solving
Other Skills:
Cooperation

MATERIALS

○ towels or small throw rugs, movement music such as calypso, reggae, or African, chart paper, markers

CHANGE THE VARIABLE

℮ Try it as a group! Using a large blanket, challenge a small group of children to become a tortoise! *How do you have to work together to move without losing the shell?*

Science Boosters

While science skills such as observing, experimenting, predicting, evaluating, inferring, and analyzing are generally thought of as left-hemisphere processes, the right hemisphere is also used in scientific thinking. Curiosity is mediated by multiple brain functions, including the right hemisphere. When you provide children with open-ended science experiments, you are inviting them to use multiple parts of the brain. Try these activities to support children's sense of discovery.

Time Flies!

BRAINWAVE.

The concept of time can be difficult for young children to grasp because it is so abstract. The connection between time and a specific event or activity makes the concept more understandable. Here is a fun way to help create temporal understanding.

HOW TO

1. Ask, *Can you see time? What do we use to tell time is passing?* Discuss how children know it is time to get up or go to bed. Point out that certain events can sometimes tell us what time it is.

2. Allow children to explore the different timers. *What do you notice about these timers?* Set two different ones to go off in one minute and see if they go off at the same time.

3. Invite children to experiment with estimating time. Provide a set of blocks and ask children to predict how many they can put in a big box before the one-minute bell rings.

4. Record children's predictions and then test them. Reverse it and ask children how many minutes it will take them to build a tower. Predict, record, and test.

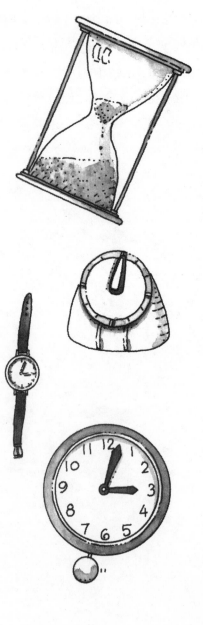

SKILLS

Observing
Flexible thinking
Predicting
Estimating

MATERIALS

✿ different types of timers, such as an egg timer, hourglass, wind-up kitchen timer, stop watch, wristwatch, or clock, chart paper, markers

CHANGE THE VARIABLE

☙ Make a sand timer by putting a small hole in the bottom of a paper cup, then set it in the mouth of a large jar and fill it with sand. See how long it takes for all the sand to run out of the cup. Make the hole bigger and have children predict whether it will take more or less time to drain!

☙ Time a variety of familiar activities. *How long does it take to sing "This Old Man"? to play a certain board game? to wash up for lunch?*

Thought Bubbles

BRAINWAVE. Problem solving is a great stimulator for the brain. The process of solving open-ended problems stimulates synaptic growth and inspires children to use higher-order thinking skills.

HOW TO

1. Make bubbles with the bubble solution. Invite children to observe the bubbles as they are made. *What do you notice about the bubbles? What shapes, sizes, and colors do you see? Are all the bubbles the same? What happens to the bubbles when they touch something?*

2. Discuss the science of bubble making together. *What makes bubbles? When have you seen bubbles in your house? What made them? How can we make bubbles?*

3. Provide different soap products for children to experiment with. Allow plenty of time for them to try mixing and testing different bubble solutions. *Which soap makes the best bubbles?*

SKILLS

Problem solving
Observing
Predicting
Flexible thinking
Inferring

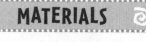

MATERIALS

- commercial bubble solution, bubble wands, a variety of different soap products (detergent, bar soap, powdered soap, a good-quality liquid dishwashing detergent), dishpans

CHANGE THE VARIABLE

- Ask, *How many different types of bubbles can we blow?* Provide wands, berry baskets, string loops, colanders, anything with holes for children to test out. *What makes the biggest bubble? What makes the smallest?*

- Add a few drops of glycerin to give bubbles more elasticity!

43

Color Craze

BRAINWAVE. In infancy, children are drawn to the stark differences of black and white. By the early childhood years, the brain perceives a wide variety of colors—and is attracted to and stimulated by them.

HOW TO

1. Invite children to help you put a few drops of red food coloring in a cup. Repeat with two more cups, using blue and yellow.

2. Provide absorbent paper towels or coffee filters for children to experiment on. Show them how to dip into the colored water with the towel or coffee filter, dipping a corner or end in the dye bath and watching it spread, then dipping it again in a different cup of color.

3. Encourage children to talk about the colors they are making. *What do you notice about the colors? What happens when the colors touch?* Help children notice the new colors they have created. *What are some of the new colors you have made? What happened when the blue touched the red?*

4. Provide cups of clear water for children to experiment with their "recipes" by making cups of new colors.

SKILLS

Problem solving
Observing
Predicting
Inferring
Flexible thinking

MATERIALS

- red, blue, and yellow food coloring, paper towels or coffee filters, clear plastic cups of water

CHANGE THE VARIABLE

- Have children mix colors using different media. Provide red, blue, and yellow in paints or with sheets of cellophane paper, or try mixing two color globs of playdough.

Boats That Float

BRAINWAVE.

Experiences with new materials or problems encourage children to use their brains to process information in new ways. This exercise develops the most important muscle of the body . . . the brain!

HOW TO

1 Invite children to brainstorm things they think boats might be made of. Show the collection of materials and ask, *How many of these materials can float like a boat? Does paper float? foam? wood? Let's make boats to see!*

2 Allow children to experiment with different designs. As they experiment, ask, *Does your boat float or sink? Why do you think it sank? How can you help it float?*

3 Expand the experience by providing marbles, beans, or other manipulatives as "cargo" for the boat. *How many marbles can your boat hold without sinking?*

SKILLS

Problem solving
Observing
Predicting
Flexible thinking

MATERIALS

✿ a collection of materials children can use to make boats (egg cartons, juice containers, craft sticks, disposable foam food trays and Styrofoam pieces, wood scraps, foil, cardboard, clay or play-dough, plastic wrap, plain paper), water table or container, marbles, beans or small manipulatives

CHANGE THE VARIABLE

✐ Change the materials— try balls of clay. *Will it float? What happens when the clay ball is shaped like a boat?*

Melting Magic

BRAINWAVE The concept of change is a major part of scientific exploration and understanding. Often, science experiments deal with changing matter and then observing the results. When children participate in these sorts of activities, they stimulate brain development.

HOW TO

1. Show an ice cube and ask, *Where or when have you seen ice? What does it do? What do you think makes ice melt?*

2. Bring out the "ice pies" and invite children to brainstorm ways they could melt the ice. *What do we need to make the ice melt? Are there some places in the room or outdoors where the ice will melt faster than in others?* Write their predictions on chart paper.

3. Have children choose several different spaces to put the pans so that the ice can begin to melt. (Try putting one in a refrigerator or outside on a cold day for comparison!) Check on them frequently during the day. *What is happening? Which is melting the fastest? Why?*

SKILLS

Problem solving
Observing
Predicting
Flexible thinking

MATERIALS

○ aluminum pie pans filled with water and then frozen to make "ice pies," chart paper, markers

CHANGE THE VARIABLE

● Show children some table salt. *Have you ever seen snowplows sprinkle salt? Why do you think they do so? What would happen if we sprinkled salt on an ice pie? What if we mixed the salt with some water and poured in on? Try it and see!*

● *What else will melt in the warm sun?* Try chocolate, butter, a birthday candle, crayons, and so on!

Water Magnifiers

BRAINWAVE Finding new uses for familiar things is fascinating to children! With this activity, experimenting with the magnifying properties of water helps the brain add dimension to its current understanding.

HOW TO

1. Give children time to experiment with the magnifying glasses and the objects. Invite them to tell you what they notice. *What happens when you look through the magnifier? How do things look different?* Have them explore the room with the magnifier.

2. In your water table or basins, place the plastic bags and the pitchers of water and invite children to explore what they can do with these items. *How can we use the water in the plastic bags to make objects look bigger?* Encourage them to try filling and sealing the bags, and using them like the magnifier. *Do things look bigger when you look through the water?*

3. Invite children to take their "magnifying bags" around the room to test out their creation! Suggest that they experiment with different amounts of water in the bag.

SKILLS

Problem solving
Observing
Predicting
Inferring

MATERIALS

- plastic basins, small water cans or pitchers, plastic magnifying glasses, resealable plastic bags, and small, interesting objects (shells, marbles, coins, feathers, and so on)

CHANGE THE VARIABLE

- Have children add food coloring or soap to the water, or use a different-sized bag. *What happens?*

- Invite children to put a small object in a bowl, loosely stretch plastic wrap over the top, and fill the bowl with water. *Does the object look bigger?*

Sound Off!

BRAINWAVE.  The brain is enthralled with sound. Make a sound and everyone turns around! Sound is one of the first stimuli to which an infant responds; A baby knows the sound of his mother's voice or even his father's footsteps coming down the hall. Sound is important for young children to experiment with, since it helps them make important sensory-motor connections.

HOW TO

1. Request that children listen to the sounds they hear in the room. *What do you hear? What sounds are in the room? What sounds might be outside the room?*

2. Invite children to play a sound guessing game. Go behind the screen or bookcase and make the sound of one of the objects you have collected. *What could it be?* If children are having difficulty identifying the sound, give them some simple clues: Describe how it is used or what it looks like.

3. Ask a child to go behind the screen and make a sound using one of the objects. *What is it? How do you know what it is without seeing it?* Make sure that after the sound is guessed, the child shows the object and makes the sound again so that a visual connection is made with the auditory experience.

SKILLS

Problem solving
Observing
Comparing
Predicting
Sensory-motor

MATERIALS

- a collection of objects that make sounds (familiar and unfamiliar), a screen or bookcase

CHANGE THE VARIABLE

- Children can make their own sound shakers by filling cylindrical film containers with pebbles, beans, sand, and so on. Have them make two of each to match and then challenge their classmates to guess what they've filled them with!

Let the Sun Shine In

BRAINWAVE. Concepts that don't fit an expected pattern are stimulating to the brain. When children's experiences are contradictory to a preconceived notion, the brain becomes fully engaged in sorting out the information and expanding to make room for the new information.

HOW TO

1. Ask children to look around the room for examples of sun shining in the room. Do you notice anything through which the sunlight is shining? Point out curtains, pictures on the window, fish tanks, shades, and so on.

2. Ask, *Will the sun shine through a rock? a leaf? paper? fabric?* Record each prediction on a chart in one of two columns: yes (green) and no (red).

3. Bring out your collection of different rocks, papers, leaves, and so on, and have children test their hypotheses.

4. Refer back to the prediction chart to see if their findings match. *What do you notice about the different rocks? What about the leaves? Why did the light shine through some but not others? What is the same or different about these objects?*

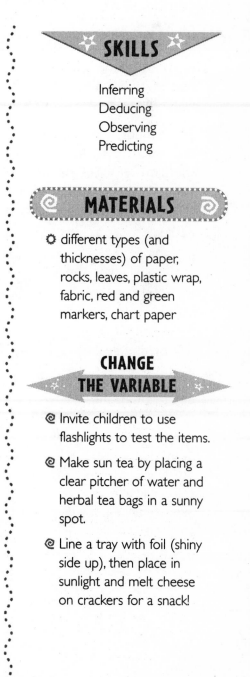

SKILLS

Inferring
Deducing
Observing
Predicting

MATERIALS

- different types (and thicknesses) of paper, rocks, leaves, plastic wrap, fabric, red and green markers, chart paper

CHANGE THE VARIABLE

- Invite children to use flashlights to test the items.
- Make sun tea by placing a clear pitcher of water and herbal tea bags in a sunny spot.
- Line a tray with foil (shiny side up), then place in sunlight and melt cheese on crackers for a snack!

Cause and Effect

BRAINWAVE. Organizing information into usable sequences is one way the brain makes sense of all the information it receives every second. Cognitive organizers are an excellent way to help children "see" their own thoughts. Adding this dimension takes children's experiences to a higher level of thinking and abstraction.

HOW TO

1. Put out toys for children to experiment with. Invite them to notice all the possible reactions that happen when they take an action.

2. Show children an if-then cognitive organizer (see below). Invite them to brainstorm logic problems using this visual-thinking device. For example: Draw clouds in the IF box and ask, *What if there were clouds in the sky? What might happen next?*

3. Encourage children to brainstorm a list of possible effects (it might rain, we might not go out for recess, there will be puddles).

4. Now invite children to think of something to put in the IF box. *What if there was no more televisions or computers? What if dinosaurs came back to life?* Complete the organizer again.

SKILLS

Inferring
Deducing
Predicting
Determining cause and effect

MATERIALS

○ cause-and-effect toys such as balls and ramps, hammer boards, or push-the-button games, chart paper, marker

CHANGE THE VARIABLE

◎ Try some logic predictions before you go on a class walk or a trip. *If we go to the woods, what might we see?*

◎ Play logic activities with block ramps and toy trucks. Invite children to predict where the truck will go if it is rolled down the ramp.

Gravity Games

BRAINWAVE

Some concepts may be too abstract for children to fully grasp at this age, but they are still enthralling enough to "fire up" the brain and cause important processing to occur. Don't be afraid to introduce difficult topics such as gravity. As long children have some hands-on experiences they will be developing their understanding.

HOW TO

1. Give children a concrete experience with gravity. Hold up a book and ask, *What will happen if I let go of the book? Will it go up or down?* Drop the book to demonstrate. *Why did it go down?* Explain that gravity is pulling on the book to make it fall.

2. Try some experiments with gravity outdoors. Drop some of the different objects and observe the fall. *What do you notice?*

3. Have children jump from a stair, go down a slide, ride a seesaw, or hang upside down from the climbing bars to physically feel the pull of gravity on their bodies. Ask children to time how long they can hold their hands over their heads. *Why do your arms get tired?* Invite children to jump as high as they can. *Why can't you jump off Earth into space?*

SKILLS

Observing
Comparing
Inferring

MATERIALS

- small objects of different weights (books, pieces of paper, rocks, feathers, and so on)

CHANGE THE VARIABLE

- Play some gravity-related games with ramps and balls, marble-roll mazes, and yo-yos. *How would these games be different if there was no gravity?*

- Invite children to move to music as they try to keep balloons (not helium-filled!) floating in the air.

Math Boosters

What helps children develop math skills? Much of math processing is the responsibility of the left hemisphere of the brain. Matching, sorting, sequencing, and patterning, as well as computation skills, are found here. Spatial awareness, primarily a function of the right hemisphere, is also a part of math functioning. These activities are designed to bridge the two hemispheres and address the math development needs of the whole child. For children, the fun and interest is in the materials, which invite them to see the usefulness of math in everyday life.

Graph It!

BRAINWAVE.

Another way to help the brain sort information is by using cognitive organizers. A simple picture graph or bar graph is one of the first ways children learn how to organize information and make comparisons of more than, less than, and equal to.

HOW TO

1. Invite children to look around and quickly estimate, without counting, how many chairs are in the room. Record their estimates on chart paper.

2. Give a bunch of sticky notes (in the same color) to one child to place on each chair. Have other children repeat with other items in the room, such as tables, windows, and doors (use a different color sticky note for each category).

3. Show children the bar graph and invite them to name the object in each bar. *Now we can use the stickers to help us count. We put the red stickers on all the chairs. Let's bring them back and put them in the chairs column on the graph. Then we will count and see how many we have!* Repeat the process for all the objects on the graph.

4. When all the sticky notes are collected and placed on the graph, ask children to "read" the results. *Let's count the stickers in each column. Which item did we find the most of? Which item had the smallest number of stickers? Are there more chairs than tables? What else do you notice?* Compare the results with the earlier estimates. *How close were the guesses?*

SKILLS

Observing
Comparing
Other Skills:
Counting
Graphing

MATERIALS

- chart paper or large-square graph paper, sticky notes in different colors, crayons

  (In advance, draw a simple chair, door, table, and window across the bottom of a piece of chart paper; these will form the base of a bar graph.)

CHANGE THE VARIABLE

- If you can count it, you can graph it! Use bar graphs to count the number of different types of vehicles that go by the playground, the different types of shoes children wear, and various types of blocks, trucks, or dolls in the room.

53

Pairing Off

BRAINWAVE.
The brain likes to organize information and make connections. The process of matching things according to their use or function builds inference and deduction skills.

HOW TO

1. Place the collected pairs of items in the pillowcase. Invite a child to take an object out of the bag, name it, and discuss how it might be used.

2. That child passes the bag to the next child, who does the same. *What do you know about this object?* Keep passing the bag around the circle until it is empty.

3. Show one object and ask, *Can you find something that goes with this object? Why do these two objects go together?*

4. Invite children to use the two items in a story!

SKILLS

Matching
Classifying
Inferring
Deducing
Expressive and receptive language
Problem solving

MATERIALS

- pillowcase, sets of objects that go together in some way such as shoe and sock, crayon and paper, cup and saucer, fork and spoon, doll and doll clothes, toy train and track

CHANGE THE VARIABLE

- Take a walk to find pairs of things in nature.

- Invite children to bring from home two things that go together in a pair.

- Put pairs of things in the dramatic play corner for children to match (shoes, socks, mittens, gloves).

Cover It Up!

BRAINWAVE
Although the concept of area is often taught in upper elementary grades, young children can begin to understand it with hands-on experience. Research shows that explorations with shape and structure help children develop the spatial skills necessary for higher-order math thinking.

HOW TO

1. Place cardboard shapes on the floor in your block area or on a math table and challenge children to cover the shapes with building blocks. *See if you can cover the shape using any size blocks you want, without leaving empty space, or having blocks hang over the edge.*

2. After they have experimented with filling up the shapes, invite children to notice the number of blocks needed to fill each. *Which shapes need the most blocks? Which type of block was the easiest to use?*

3. Now ask children to take those blocks off and try to fill the shapes again with different blocks. *Will you need the same number of blocks you needed before? Try it and see!*

SKILLS

Observing
Comparing
Flexible thinking
Problem solving
Estimating

MATERIALS

✿ blocks, masking tape, large cardboard or oaktag shapes (squares, rectangles, triangles), boxes of different sizes

CHANGE THE VARIABLE

@ Children can further experiment with area by attempting to fill areas of the room with sheets of newspaper. *How many will you need to fill the circle time area?*

A Handful of Thinking

BRAINWAVE. The brain has an amazing capacity to rapidly take in information. The information is then quickly interpreted, used, and discarded or stored for later use. Activities that invite children to look at something and hastily make an estimation encourage brain development. While children's estimates may be wild at first, through experience you will notice their closer and closer approximations.

HOW TO

1) Put one collection of small objects, such as beans, in a large bowl. Invite children to examine the beans in the bowl. *How many do you think you can pick up in one hand at once? Try it!* Children can say the number they estimate aloud or write it on a construction-paper mat. They then take a handful of small objects and put it on their mat.

2) Have children count to check their estimate. *Did you estimate more than, less than, or the right amount of beans? Try it again and see if you pick up the same amount.*

3) Put out a different set of small objects that are a bit smaller or larger than the first and ask children to estimate again with the new objects. *Do you think you will pick up more or less items this time? Why?*

SKILLS

Observing
Estimating
Memory
Other Skills:
Numeration

MATERIALS

- a collection of small objects (beans, keys, buttons, stones, counters, and so on), large bowl or tub, construction paper, crayons or markers

CHANGE THE VARIABLE

- Play a "guess the jellybeans in the jar" game, then have children count them in groups of ten into a muffin tin.

- Invite children to estimate how many steps it is to the door or the playground. Then, take a walk and see!

Measure Me!

BRAINWAVE

When children experience math concepts through the manipulation of real and interesting objects, they are better able to apply the skill in a variety of situations, even with materials not encountered in the first experience.

HOW TO

1. Invite children to experiment with nonstandard measurement. You might say, *Guess what? You have a tool for measuring built right into your body. Your hands!*

2. Put an object out for children to examine. *How many of your hands long is it? Let's first guess and then try it and see.*

3. Have children practice measuring other things in the room with their hands. You can record their estimations and results on the chart paper.

4. After children have measured with their hands, they can try measuring with their bodies! Cut a piece of yarn the same length as each child is tall. Invite them to go on a "measuring treasure hunt" and see how many things they can find that are as tall or long as they are!

SKILLS

Observing
Comparing
Predicting
Creative thinking

MATERIALS

✿ yarn, markers or crayons, chart paper

CHANGE THE VARIABLE

✎ Trace children's feet to use as rulers.

What Size Is It?

BRAINWAVE We've all heard the comment "everything is relative." Size certainly is, especially to young children. It can be difficult for them to grasp that something can be big in one situation and small in another. By providing children with many opportunities to experiment with relative size, you are supporting their developing ability to be able to hold all those concepts at once!

HOW TO

1. Have children help you make a list of all the big things they can think of! Ask, *Which of these things is the biggest? Which is the smallest of the big things we listed? Is it still big?*

2. Introduce the concepts of big, bigger, and biggest. Select the smallest object and then invite a child to take the object that is just a little bit bigger and place it next to the smallest object. Repeat until all the objects are put in size order.

3. Point out that as the objects were being added to the line, the thing that was bigger or biggest at the time is no longer so after the next item is added. Continue the activity by inviting children to find things around the room that are bigger than the largest object in line.

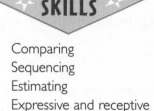

SKILLS

Comparing
Sequencing
Estimating
Expressive and receptive
  language

MATERIALS

❂ ten objects such as toys, blocks, apples, and balls (each should be just a bit bigger than its predecessor)

CHANGE THE VARIABLE

❧ Put collections of graduated-size objects (keys, crayons, buttons, rocks) for children to place in a series in the math area.

One Rotten Apple

BRAINWAVE

Even though the concept of probability isn't taught until much later in school, young children can experience it through a fun, hands-on game.

HOW TO

1. Lay out the 15 apples or cards in a row, putting the "rotten" apple at the right end of the line.

2. Explain that the object of the game is to avoid the rotten apple. Children alternate turns taking away from the row one, two, or three apples at a time. The trick is to look ahead and see how many are left so that the other player has to pick up the rotten one at the end. (Most children will randomly take away apples at first, but through experience with the game they will begin to see the pattern of what is happening and watch to see how they can arrange things so that another player gets the bad apple.)

3. Play the game several times in a row so that children get an opportunity to see the strategy.

SKILLS

Sequencing
Patterning
Predicting/Estimating
Other Skills:
Probability
Strategy
Left to right progression

MATERIALS

- 15 real apples (or any other fruit) or 15 index cards with pictures of apples (put an X or a drawing or sticker of a worm on one of the apples or cards)

CHANGE THE VARIABLE

- Use other objects to play the game, or go outside and play it using rocks.

- Make the line shorter by using fewer items, or longer by using more items.

People Patterns

BRAINWAVE.

Patterns help the brain "see" connections and relationships. Patterning is also an essential math skill, basic to comparing, estimating, counting, adding, and subtracting. When manipulating real objects, children deepen their understanding of the process of patterning.

HOW TO

1. Lay out a simple "A-B-A"-style pattern of shapes or blocks on the floor, such as circle, square, circle; circle, square, circle. "Read" and say the pattern together.

2. Ask, *What will come next in the pattern?* Have children add appropriate objects to extend the line.

3. Ask, *Can we make patterns with people?* Have three or more volunteers make an "A-B-A" pattern line. For example, one child can stand, the next can sit, the next can stand, and so on. Invite children to add themselves to the line in the correct pattern. Then have them say the pattern as they count off: *stand, sit, stand, stand, sit, stand,* and so on.

4. Try other people patterns: hands up and hands down, arms out and arms crossed, a boy-girl pattern, and so on.

SKILLS

Observing
Comparing
Patterning
Other Skills:
Counting

MATERIALS

❂ blocks or other small, easily counted manipulatives

CHANGE THE VARIABLE

❧ Children can use props to make people-pattern lines in new ways. Have them use hats and other costumes to mark the differences between "A" from "B."

❧ Try more difficult patterns, such as "A-B-C" or "A-B-B-A"!

Pattern Path

BRAINWAVE. When movement is added to children's acquisition of a concept, they gain deeper experience and understanding of it. Have you ever found that an idea becomes clearer to you as you walk? Add the kinesthetic modality to a math experience, and see children's understanding soar!

HOW TO

(1) Put a pattern of cardboard shapes (such as circle, square, circle, square) on the floor. Point to each shape and say its name. Invite children to join you in saying the names of shapes.

(2) Create a "pattern path" by taping the shapes on the floor in an open area suitable for movement. Invite a child to step on the shapes as the others help him or her say or beat the pattern with claps or rhythm sticks.

(3) Expand the experience by inviting children to walk backward through the pattern path. *Can you say the pattern backward? Is it the same as it is when it is said forward?*

SKILLS

Patterning
Observing
Comparing
Perceptual-motor
Other Skills:
Counting
Following directions

MATERIALS

✿ rhythm sticks, large cardboard shapes (circles, squares, triangles), masking tape

CHANGE THE VARIABLE

◉ Children can also make up a pattern of arm movements to go with their steps along the path (right hand in the air, left hand in the air, and so on).

There Are Many Ways to See It

BRAINWAVE. The brain responds to diversity with curiosity. Looking at things in multiple ways is an essential part of learning. In particular, experimenting with sorting and classifying objects in different ways encourages independent and flexible thinking, and expands the mind's capacity to consider options.

HOW TO

1. Give children a set of objects, such as buttons, for children to examine. *How are these items the same? How are they different?* Invite children to discuss what they notice, and have them organize items (by color, shape, size, or any other attribute they can think of) onto the different plates.

2. After children have sorted the objects in one way, ask them to gather the objects together again and sort them in a new way. *How else are these items the same or different? How many ways can you sort these?*

SKILLS

Classifying
Flexible thinking
Creative thinking
Other Skills:
Graphing

MATERIALS

- set of small objects (keys, spoons, buttons), paper plates

CHANGE THE VARIABLE

- Invite children to apply the sorting process to their environment. Ask them to sort objects they find in the classroom (crayons, blocks) or in nature (leaves, rocks).

- Invite children to notice what is the same or different about one another's shoes.

Notes

Notes